About
What We See
in a Catholic Church

Les Miller

NOVALIS

© 2011 Novalis Publishing Inc.

Cover design: Mardigrafe
Cover illustration: Audrey Wells
Interior images: pp. 12, 31, 49: W.P. Wittman; p. 15: Karoli Dombi;
pp. 19, 21, 37, 39, 41: Plaisted; p. 46: Ingram
Layout: Mardigrafe and Audrey Wells

Published by Novalis

Publishing Office
10 Lower Spadina Avenue, Suite 400
Toronto, Ontario, Canada
M5V 2Z2

Head Office
4475 Frontenac Street
Montréal, Québec, Canada
H2H 2S2

www.novalis.ca

Library and Archives Canada Cataloguing in Publication

Miller, Les, 1952-
        25 questions about what we see in a Catholic church /
        Les Miller.

ISBN 978-2-89646-322-0

        1. Catholic church buildings--Juvenile literature.
2. Catholic Church--Liturgical objects--Juvenile literature. I. Title.
II. Title: Twenty-five questions about what we see in a Catholic church.

BX1970.3.M55 2011   j246'.9582   C2011-901608-7

Printed in Canada.

We acknowledge the financial support of the Government of Canada through
the Canada Book Fund for business development activities.

5   4   3   2   1   15   14   13   12   11

TABLE OF CONTENTS

A word from the author

From the minute you step inside the doors of a Catholic church, you can worship and learn without hearing a single word spoken. Our Catholic churches are full of symbols and teachings. Symbols are found in the design of the church itself, the furniture, the windows, the decorations and even in the cloths used on the altar.

Some of the symbols are easy to figure out, but others have a deeper story to tell. It is my hope that this book will help make going to church a richer experience for you. If we know the symbolism of many of these features, we may better understand the story behind them.

This book starts by looking at some general questions about what churches are for. Then we enter the church, move to the main part of the building, look around the altar, then go outside the church. We even look at who goes to church. Next time you go to church, take this book with you and use it as a guide to see how many of the features you can find.

I am dedicating this book to my children and godchildren: Victoria, Sarah, Joe, Anthony, David and Matthew. May they keep asking questions and finding answers that lead them deeper into God's love. And may they (and you!) find in this book a path to a deeper relationship with the Church.

Les Miller

Why do Catholics go to church?

*G*oing to church is a key part of being Catholic. When our Church leaders gathered at the *Second Vatican Council* in the 1960s, they called the Eucharist "the source and summit of our faith." The Eucharist brings us into a deeper relationship with God.

Although we also need to pray on our own, it isn't enough. We need to praise God with others. That's why we celebrate Mass as a community. As Catholics, we believe that we were made to serve each other and to worship together. Jesus told us that when we gather together like this, he is present. We come together to worship, even though none of us is perfect. Because the Eucharist is a sacrament, we sense God's love in a deep way at Mass.

When we go to Mass, we learn more about our faith. We hear the scriptures, we proclaim the creed together, and we tell God our needs in prayer. We also listen to the priest or deacon's homily after the Gospel. The homily helps us see what God's word means for us in our lives today.

Celebrating Mass together helps us bring God's love to others in the community. Some people from the church community visit the sick or the homebound. Others work with the poor, the homeless and the troubled. Those who work in schools and hospitals also gain spiritual strength for their work. In our everyday lives, no matter how old we are, we are asked to bring God's love and spirit into whatever we do.

Going to Mass on Sundays is one of the duties of being a Catholic. In fact, Canadians have 54 "days of obligation": each Sunday of the year plus Christmas Day and the feast of Mary, Mother of God (New Year's Day). But we are encouraged to go to Mass as often as we can.

The first Eucharistic celebration was the Last Supper, when Jesus celebrated his final meal with his disciples. During this meal he taught his disciples, washed their feet in an act of service, and shared the bread and wine with them. He asked them to remember him in the breaking of bread and the drinking of wine, which we do in the Eucharist.

For more about the Eucharist, see *25 Questions about the Mass*.

What is the difference between a cathedral and a church?

The original word for "church" (*ecclesia* in Greek) meant the gathering of people, not a building. The early Christians gathered wherever they could – often in people's homes and sometimes in secret caves. It was often dangerous for them to meet because Christianity was against the law in the Roman Empire. As things got safer and the Roman Empire became Christian, buildings were set aside as gathering places. Soon the word for the community became the word for where the community would gather.

The leader of the earliest community was the Bishop. But as the church spread, there were not enough Bishops to go around. After a few centuries, the Bishop passed on the leadership of many of these churches to priests. The Bishop still had special responsibilities for the churches in that area, including teaching and making important decisions. When he did these things, he was said to speak from his chair, or *cathedra*. This was a sign of the Bishop's authority. The church where he worshipped was called the cathedral.

These cathedrals tended to be found in major cities and were usually the largest and most elaborate places of worship in the area. They were often the pride of the city and were built to last for centuries. Notre Dame in Paris and Santiago de Compostela in Spain are many centuries old. Special ceremonies are often held in cathedrals, such as the ordination of Bishops, priests and deacons, as well as royal weddings and funerals.

 Cathedra is a Latin word for a chair with armrests.

 In churches, the seat where the priest sits is called the *presidential chair*. This has nothing to do with a political office. "Presidential" means "one who presides." In the case of a priest, he presides at the Mass.

 Other large churches are called *basilicas*. This word was originally used for large Roman public buildings. Some of these buildings were later used for Christian worship. Not all basilicas are cathedrals. St. Joseph's Oratory is a basilica but not the cathedral church of Montreal. In that city, Notre Dame Cathedral holds the *cathedra* of the Archbishop.

Where are people baptized?

Do you remember the story of the baptism of Jesus in the Bible? His cousin, John, baptized him in the Jordan River. Christians celebrate their entry into the faith by being baptized, just as Jesus was baptized. If you have ever been to a baptism, chances are it wasn't at a local river or lake! Christianity spread to places where it wasn't practical to put people into rivers, so pools were built in a separate building called a baptistery next to the church. Over time, these pools were built smaller and smaller, and were placed in the church itself. In many Catholic churches today, these are large basins called *fonts*. This is where the priest or deacon baptizes new members of the church.

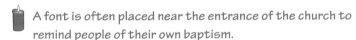

A font is often placed near the entrance of the church to remind people of their own baptism.

The formal name for the entrance of the church is the *narthex*.

You can read more about the symbolism of water and other baptismal symbols in *25 Questions about Catholic Signs and Symbols*.

Why is there a bowl of water near the entrance?

Some churches also have small bowls (called *stoups*) containing water just inside the church doors. On our way in or out, we dip our fingertips in the water and then bless ourselves by making the sign of the cross. This action reminds us of our baptism and the promises to live as Jesus taught us.

The water used in stoups and fonts is called holy water. It is blessed at the Easter Vigil when the large Easter or Paschal candle is lit and then the bottom of the candle is dipped in the water. The Paschal candle represents Jesus, the Light of the world. It is sometimes called the Christ candle.

Stoups are often designed in the form of a shell. This is ancient Christian symbolism. Shells connect us with the fishing work that several of Jesus' disciples did. Jesus promised the disciples that when they left their nets behind, they would be fishers of people. The scallop shell became a symbol for pilgrims who were searching for greater faith. In a sense, all of us are pilgrims. We are seeking better relationships with God, with each other and with our true selves.

Shells were also used to baptize people. Using the shell, the priest would pour three drops of water over the baptized person's head, one drop for each person of the Blessed Trinity (Father, Son and Holy Spirit).

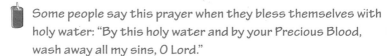

Holy water is also sprinkled on us as part of the Easter liturgies and at other key times during the church year. The *aspergillum* (Latin for "sprinkler") is dipped in a small bowl of holy water. The priest then flicks water over the people to remind them of their baptism.

Some people say this prayer when they bless themselves with holy water: "By this holy water and by your Precious Blood, wash away all my sins, O Lord."

At one time in early Church history, a church minister sprinkled water on the people as they entered the church.

What do we call the seats at church?

Inside most churches there are seats or benches called *pews*. (Some churches use chairs, which can be moved around and set up in different ways.) We think the word "pew" comes from the Latin word *podium*, which is a raised place. Nowadays we all sit in pews, but if we were to go back 500 years, we would find that only the rich were given places to sit on raised benches. Most people had to stand or kneel on the floor.

Most churches have places where we can kneel to pray. These are called kneeling benches or kneelers. Kneeling is a prayer position that shows humility. It shows that worshippers are sorry for their sins. It also shows deep love or adoration for God.

Usually, a rack on each pew holds books that can help us follow the liturgy. Hymnals give us the words and music notes to join in the singing. Missals contain the prayers and readings for the Mass.

 Before we sit down for the first time, and as we leave once Mass is over, it is our custom to *genuflect*: facing the tabernacle at the front of the church, we go down on one knee. (At this time, some people make the sign of the cross.) You can also pray on your knees on the kneeler at your place.

Standing is a way of showing honour. For example, if the queen, prime minister or other dignitary comes into a room, it is polite to stand and show that person respect. At certain times during the Mass, such as the reading of the Gospel and the praying of the Our Father, we all stand.

？？？？？？？？？？？ 6 ？？？？？？？？？

What do we   call the area
where most people sit?

Most people sit in pews facing the altar. This area is called the nave, from the Latin word for ship: *navis*. Some people think of the Church as a ship of faith. This very old image comes from the story of Noah's Ark in the Bible. In many traditional churches, the nave is split down the middle by an aisle. The priest and other ministers walk in a procession down this central aisle.

 In some modern churches, the pews may be arranged in a semi-circle or a full circle around the altar. People can see not only the altar, but also other people in the church. This arrangement draws attention to the community at worship. In this style of church, there may be several aisles, but there is still a central aisle.

(7)

Why are there statues or pictures showing the trial and crucifixion of Jesus?

Around the church you will see a set of 14 or 15 scenes showing the arrest, trial, punishment, crucifixion and burial of Jesus. These paintings, sculptures or reliefs (a cross between a painting and sculpture) are called the Stations of the Cross or the Way of the Cross. They help worshippers to pray about these important events in the life of Jesus. You will often see the scene accompanied by a number or Roman numeral with a brief description, such as "IV: Jesus meets his mother."

Here is a list of the traditional Stations of the Cross:

1. Jesus is condemned to death
2. Jesus takes up his cross
3. Jesus falls for the first time
4. Jesus meets his mother
5. Simon helps Jesus carry the cross
6. Veronica wipes Jesus' face
7. Jesus falls for the second time
8. The women of Jerusalem weep for Jesus
9. Jesus falls for the third time
10. Jesus is stripped of his garments
11. Jesus is nailed to the cross
12. Jesus dies on the cross
13. Jesus is removed from the cross
14. Jesus is placed in the tomb

These Stations of the Cross help us to imagine the steps that Jesus took on the way to his death on the cross. During Lent and at other times, we follow the path of Jesus from his arrest to his burial. At each stop on the path, the leader describes the events that happened at that station. We offer prayers about the meaning of the station for us today.

As we walk from one station to the next, this ritual becomes a kind of pilgrimage. A pilgrimage is a journey to a holy place. We are told that the earliest Christians followed the path from Pontius Pilate's house to the place of Jesus' crucifixion on Calvary. By praying the Stations of the Cross, we are linked with the early followers of Jesus.

At different times in history, there have been more or fewer stations. The most common number is 14. In recent times, some churches have added a 15th station: the Resurrection of Jesus.

At each station, we may pray these words: "We adore you, O Christ, and we praise you… Because, by your holy cross, you have redeemed the world."

Some churches have outdoor Stations of the Cross. These give people a deep sense of being on a pilgrimage. Some people pray the Stations of the Cross on their own at home.

Some of the events in the traditional Stations of the Cross, such as the story about Veronica giving Jesus a cloth for his face, are not found in the Bible. Pope John Paul II suggested a different version, called the scriptural Stations of the Cross:

1. Jesus in the Garden of Gethsemane
2. Jesus is betrayed by Judas and arrested

3. Jesus is condemned by the Sanhedrin

4. Jesus is denied by Peter

5. Jesus is judged by Pilate

6. Jesus is scourged and crowned with thorns

7. Jesus bears the cross

8. Jesus is helped by Simon to carry the cross

9. Jesus meets the women of Jerusalem

10. Jesus is crucified

11. Jesus promises his kingdom to the good thief

12. Jesus speaks to his mother and the disciple

13. Jesus dies on the cross

14. Jesus is placed in the tomb

Why do churches have coloured glass windows?

Richly coloured glass windows are an impressive feature of many Catholic churches. These works of art let worshippers know they are in a place that prizes beauty. These windows are important symbols that contain Christian teachings.

Such windows may show detailed designs as well as pictures of figures such as God the Creator, Jesus Christ, the Holy Spirit, our Blessed Mother Mary, the saints and other holy people. Sometimes the windows show key Bible scenes, such as the baptism, crucifixion and resurrection of Jesus. These scenes come to life when light shines through them. The light is a powerful symbol. We read in the Bible that God created light and that Jesus is the Light of the world. The scenes and the light reveal the sacred.

Scenes from the Bible and images of holy people were used to teach and remind people of stories about their faith. When most people could not read, they learned about God through stories. The glass windows illustrated these stories for all.

One way to create colours in the window is to stain the molten glass by adding chemicals and dyes to it. With painted glass, the colour did not last nearly as long.

Some stained glass windows have a circular pattern. These are called rose windows, not only because they resemble the flower, but also because the rose is a symbol of the Blessed Virgin Mary.

Some of these windows did such a good job of telling stories from Scripture that they were called the Poor Man's Bible.

9

Why are there statues or pictures of Mary in the church?

Like stained glass windows, statues remind us of important figures or events in sacred history. Most churches have a statue of the Blessed Virgin Mary. Catholics often use these statues to focus their prayers, asking Mary to pray with them or for them to God.

Jesus is our Saviour, but Mary, his mother, also plays a major role in the story of God's love for us. Mary carried the Son of God in her womb for nine months. Can you imagine this responsibility? Because her courage, devotion and wisdom are a model of living for all people, we have a special respect and love for her. She is our mother, too.

Some statues show Mary at important moments during her life:

• Our Lady of the Annunciation – when the Angel Gabriel told her she was to give birth to the Son of God.

• Mary, Mother of God – when she gave birth to Jesus. Sometimes this is shown as the Madonna and child.

• Mary, Queen of Sorrows – when she received the dead body of her son at the crucifixion.

• Mary, Queen of the Apostles – when she was present at Pentecost, when the Holy Spirit came to her and the disciples.

Prayers that people pray at a statue of Mary include the Hail Mary, the Hail, Holy Queen, and the rosary. (For more about these prayers, see *25 Questions about Catholic Signs and Symbols* and *25 Questions about Prayer.*)

In your parish church, you might also find statues of the patron of your church and of St. Joseph, patron saint of Canada.

Mary has appeared to people a number of times, including to St. Juan Diego at Guadeloupe, Mexico, in 1531; to St. Bernadette at Lourdes, France, in 1858; and to three children at Fatima, Portugal, in 1917.

Important feast days for Mary include the Immaculate Conception (December 8); Mary, Mother of God (January 1); the Annunciation (March 25); the Assumption (August 15); and the Nativity of Mary (September 8).

10

What is the sacristy?

At a theatre, backstage is a place where things are stored and actors prepare. Churches have a similar area for storage and preparing for Mass. Priests and others who help him during Mass get ready in the *sacristy*. The priest's *vestments* are stored here. (Vestments are worn over his regular clothing.) The priest chooses the vestments with the correct colour and style for the celebration. For example, if the Mass is celebrated during Lent, the priest usually chooses purple vestments. For Ordinary Time, the vestments are green.

Several items used in the Mass are stored in the sacristy, including the cross for processions and the books of prayers and readings. The sacred vessels (such as cups and plates) as well as the altar cloths and linens used in worship are also stored here. You will always find a sink in the sacristy. That is where we wash the vessels used in the liturgy. Under church law, the drain from the sink cannot go into the sewer; it must go directly into the ground. This is to show special respect for any traces of the Body and Blood of Christ that may remain in the vessels when they are washed.

 The sacristy is usually in a side room near the altar.

 The word "sacristy" comes from the Latin word *sacra*, which means "sacred."

 The person in charge of looking after the sacristy is called a sacristan.

Why is there a cross on the wall?

One of the most noticeable features of any Catholic church is the cross. This symbol of Jesus Christ reminds us of our identity as Christians. The main purpose of a church is to bring people into deeper friendship with Jesus. We call ourselves Christians because this is the most important relationship in our lives. Jesus shows us a path of goodness and meaning in a difficult world.

If the cross has an image of the body of Christ on it, it is called a crucifix. The body may represent the crucified Christ or the risen Christ after the resurrection. Both forms of crucifix reflect important aspects of Christianity. The crucified Christ draws attention to the sacrifice of Jesus. But the crucifixion must be understood in light of the resurrection. Suffering and death are not the end. God's love continues after death. In fact, we become even closer to God after we die.

The cross and the crucifix are symbols of the most important feast for Christians: Easter. These symbols remind us of Easter every time we worship at Mass, because at each Mass we celebrate the death and resurrection of Jesus.

 St. Francis of Assisi had a vision of Jesus speaking to him from a cross in the chapel of San Damiano in Italy. The voice asked him to rebuild the church. Francis later realized that this calling was to reform the whole Church, not just to restore one building.

Crosses are everywhere in Christian symbolism. Many churches are built in the shape of a cross. Many priests' vestments and altar cloths have crosses woven into them.

What is a confessional?

Most churches have small rooms where you can speak with the priest about the problems you are facing as you try to live a good life. We know when our relationships are in trouble because our conscience bothers us. That is the time to go to the confessional or reconciliation room and talk with the priest in the sacrament of Reconciliation. Reconciliation is all about healing our relationships with God, family, friends and the community.

Confessions can be held anywhere that is private. Some people prefer confessionals. Many confessionals have a kneeler where you can kneel in prayer as you make your confession. You are separated from the priest by a wooden screen, so you cannot see each other's faces. This reminds us that we are making our confessions to God through the priest. Other people like to sit face to face with the priest in a reconciliation room. These rooms are larger than confessionals. They have a couple of chairs where you and the priest can talk together and pray. These have appeared since the Second Vatican Council, when new ideas about this sacrament were introduced.

At the beginning of Mass, we may say a form of confession together. The Confiteor is the part that starts with "I confess to almighty God and to you, my brothers and sisters …". After a while, our relationships become damaged and we need deeper healing. That is when we turn to the sacrament of Reconciliation.

Private confessions began centuries ago, when Irish monks started the practice.

As Catholics, we must "confess our sins to a priest, at least once a year" in the sacrament of Reconciliation. But we are encouraged to take part in this healing sacrament more often if we need to.

Sometimes people are nervous about telling their sins to the priest. But there is no need to worry. According to Church law, the priest is not allowed to tell anyone else what you have said.

What objects are carried in the entrance procession?

At the beginning of Mass, the priest, lectors and others walk up to the altar in a procession. Some of them carry certain objects. A cross or crucifix on top of a pole usually leads the procession. Sometimes, the first item is the *censer*, which contains incense. Both the crucifix and the censer remind us that this is a holy gathering. The altar servers may carry the candles that will be placed beside the altar. The people who read the Word of God and those who help give out communion may follow. *The Book of the Gospels* or *Lectionary* is held up high for all to see. The priest is the last person in the procession.

In a way, this procession is like a pilgrimage or a spiritual journey. We are always on our way towards God. The altar is the focus of the Mass, so those in the procession bow in front of it and genuflect facing the *tabernacle* (a small cabinet near the altar where the Body of Christ is kept). The people in the pews stand and sing a hymn to God during this opening procession.

 At some special Masses, everyone joins in the procession. In that case, the procession takes place outside the church and through the neighbourhood. One such occasion is Passion

Sunday, when worshippers carry palm branches as they walk. Another takes place at Corpus Christi (the feast when we honour the Body and Blood of Christ). Here the priest carries the host in a sacred vessel.

 The processional cross is placed near the altar and the place where the Gospel will be proclaimed.

AROUND THE ALTAR

What is the sanctuary?

When we go to Mass, our attention is usually focused on the area around the altar. This is called the *sanctuary*. It usually includes the places from which the readings are proclaimed and the prayers are prayed, the chairs where the priest and his assistants sit, and the tabernacle. The priest leads the celebration of the Mass from the sanctuary.

The sanctuary is often seen as holy ground. In fact, the word "sanctuary" comes from the Latin word *sanctus*, which means "holy." In older churches, this area may be separated from the rest of the church by three steps and an altar rail.

The sanctuary was often higher than the rest of the Church – not only so the worshippers could see the actions of the priest, but also because the raised height emphasized the holiness of the Mass. (Many of our modern churches also have a raised sanctuary.) Another sign that the sanctuary was a special place was the altar rail. Here worshippers would kneel down and receive communion directly on their tongues.

Today, we see the whole church as holy. This includes the congregation, which is part of the Body of Christ. In most of our churches, the altar rail has been removed and people stand to receive communion in their hand.

 In medieval times, people on the run from the law could claim sanctuary in a church for a period of time. As long as they didn't leave the church, they were safe. In these cases, church law came before civil law.

 In ancient Rome and other places, sanctuaries were built over the tombs of holy people. For example, St. Peter's Basilica in Vatican City is believed to be built over the tomb of St. Peter.

What do we call the place where the scriptures are proclaimed?

The scriptures, which are the Word of God, are proclaimed from the *ambo*. It is usually found near the altar and is called "the table of the Word."

The ambo usually has a graceful design to show that this is a place where words of power and beauty will be proclaimed. It often has a microphone so everyone can hear. Can you imagine how loudly the readers had to proclaim in the days before amplified sound? Notice that we are saying "proclaim" the scriptures instead of "read" the scriptures. Proclaiming is a special way of reading out loud. The priest, *deacon* or lector (the proper name for the reader) proclaims God's word clearly, slowly and respectfully. The words being proclaimed are inspired by God, so the lectors and the priest need to let people know that this is a sacred message. After the first reading is proclaimed, the psalm is often sung. (The psalm is a song from the Book of Psalms in the Bible.)

 The word "ambo" comes from a Greek word meaning *elevation*. People at the ambo often stand on a higher level than the congregation.

Because they are not the Word of God, the prayers of the faithful and church announcements are made from a *lectern*, not the ambo.

What is the altar and how is it used?

When the priest presides at Mass, he stands at a special table called an altar. But the altar is more than a table. Altars have been used in religious worship since before history was recorded. People long ago made their sacrifices

I AM WITH YOU ALWAYS

to the gods at altars. We read about altars in the Bible, too. Abraham and the Israelites used them to sacrifice animals to honour God. This tradition was continued in the Temple built in Jerusalem. Jesus taught us that his life was the final sacrifice. No more sacrifices of this kind are needed.

For Catholics, it is important that the altar look like a table. It was at a table that Jesus celebrated the Last Supper. The Mass continues this special meal focused on the table we call the altar. We place a linen cloth on the altar and have candles on each side of it.

Altars connect us with our history in another way. Within each altar is a sacred relic. A relic is an object or body part from a saint. While it may seem gruesome to know that a finger bone of a saint is in the altar, it does let us know that we are connected with holy people in a special way. Many of these saints gave their lives for their faith, which is another reminder that the altar is about sacrifice.

For Catholics, the altar is a place where we remember the sacrifice of Jesus and we eat the sacred food that is Jesus. The altar is a powerful reminder of the love of Christ.

 The altar is such a special place that it is perfumed with incense at some Masses. The priest also bows or kneels at the altar and kisses it to show respect and devotion.

 When a new church is built, the altar is specially blessed by the local Bishop.

Why are there candles on or beside the altar?

*O*ne of the most powerful symbols of Jesus is light. He told us, "I am the light of the world." (John 8:12) At times, our lives can be darkened with suffering or sadness. Things might seem hopeless. When we let Jesus into our lives, his love, joy and hope brighten that darkness. For centuries, people lit candles to lighten the darkness. It's easy to see why candles are such a powerful symbol of our faith.

Candles representing Christ's light can be found on or beside the altar and sometimes on either side of the ambo when the Word of God is proclaimed. The largest candle is the Paschal or Easter candle. A new Paschal candle is lit at the Easter Vigil celebration on Holy Saturday. Then it is lit during every Mass until Pentecost and during baptisms and funerals. People also light small votive candles as part of a special prayer, such as asking God to care for a loved one who is sick or who has died.

 Other religions also use light as an important symbol. For example, Jewish people light a menorah (a candlestick holder for eight candles) at Hanukkah, and Sabbath candles every Sabbath, on Friday evening. Hindus celebrate a festival of lights called Diwali.

The Paschal candle has the letters Alpha and Omega on it. These are the first and last letters of the Greek alphabet. They represent Christ, who is the beginning and end of all things.

Why is the altar area decorated with different colours at different times of the year?

Different times of the year make us think about different colours. We might associate winter with white because of snow, and spring with green because of new leaves on the trees. In our church year, certain colours match the different church seasons. The colours of the cloths on the altar and ambo, the decorations and the priest's clothing tell us what church season we are in.

The church year begins in Advent. This is the time when we prepare for Christmas. The colour we see most often during this time is purple. Purple has two meanings:

- It is the colour of royalty. It reminds us of the kingly nature of Jesus. One of his titles is "King of Kings."

- It is also the colour of sorrow and penance. During Advent, we look at the things that are stopping us from having healthy relationships with others and with God. We also prepare our hearts to welcome Jesus.

The main colour at Christmas is white, the colour of purity and celebration.

Between Christmas and Lent, we move into Ordinary Time. The colour for this season is green, which represents life and hope.

During Lent, a time of preparation for Easter, we see purple in our churches. Again, purple means it is a time of penance and preparation.

Lent ends with Easter. The colour for Easter is white, which means we are again celebrating purity and joy. The Easter season lasts for 50 days.

Easter ends at Pentecost. Now we see the colour red, which reminds us of the tongues of fire that appeared over the heads of the Apostles and Mary at Pentecost. This was a sign that the Holy Spirit was present.

After Pentecost, we once again see the green of Ordinary Time. It lasts until Advent, when the cycle begins all over again.

 Priests may wear rose or pink vestments on two Sundays during the church year: the Third Sunday of Advent and the

Fourth Sunday of Lent. Pink represents joy. Even in our seasons of penance, we find joy in the Christian life.

The priest might wear red at Mass on the feast day of a saint who was killed for his or her faith. These saints are called martyrs. The colour red reminds us of the blood that was shed and the faith of these holy people.

At Christmas and Easter, the priest's vestments may have gold cloth or gold trim on them. This shows that these are very special and important feasts.

What are the different cups, bowls and cloths used for?

At Mass we remember the meal Jesus shared with his friends at the Last Supper. We use certain dishes, cups, napkins and other cloths during our celebration.

The *sacred vessels* (as they are called) have deep meaning. After the Prayer of the Faithful, where we pray for the needs of the Church and the world, the altar is prepared for the Eucharist. In the Offertory Procession, someone carries up the wine in a pitcher called a *cruet*. The bread is brought forward in a *ciborium*, a bowl-like container. Near the altar is a *credence table* that holds linen cloths, a cruet of water and a bowl so the priest can wash his hands before the Eucharistic meal.

The priest continues the preparations by pouring wine and a few drops of water into a cup called a *chalice*. During the Mass, the bread in the *ciborium* is transformed into the Body of Christ and the wine (with a little water) is transformed into the Blood of Christ.

During these preparations, a number of white *altar linens* are used. The priest uses a *finger towel* to dry his hands during the preparations. A *corporeal* is used under the *ciborium* to catch any crumbs that may fall from the hosts. It is later used to clean the ciborium. A *purificator* is used to wipe the edge of the chalice after someone drinks from it.

The chalice used by Jesus has been lost. Over the centuries, many fictional stories have been told about finding it. This chalice is known as the Holy Grail.

Altar linens are first washed in a special sink that drains directly into the ground. Any traces of Christ's Body and Blood cannot be mixed with waste water.

Some priests may also use a *paten*, a vessel that looks like a saucer, to hold the sacred host.

What books are used during Mass?

During the Mass, two different books are used: the *Lectionary* and the *Sacramentary*.

The Lectionary contains the readings that are proclaimed during the first main part of the Mass, the Liturgy of the Word:

- the First Reading (usually from the Old Testament)

- the Responsorial Psalm (usually from the Book of Psalms in the Old Testament)
- the Second Reading (usually from one of the letters of the Apostles, such as St. Paul)
- the Gospel.

THE PRIEST HOLDS UP THE LECTIONARY AT MASS.

The *Sacramentary* contains the Mass prayers, such as the Opening Prayer, the Eucharistic Prayer (when the bread and wine become the Body and Blood of Jesus), and the Prayer after Communion. The Sacramentary also includes instructions for the priest, called *rubrics*, to follow as he leads the prayers. The rubrics are written in red to show that they are not to be spoken.

During the Easter Season, the first reading is from the Acts of the Apostles.

Sometimes the priest reads the Gospel from a separate book, called the Book of the Gospels. Having them in a separate book reminds us that the Gospels are central to the Christian faith. The Book of the Gospels is richly decorated and is treated with great respect.

21

What is the place where the remaining hosts are stored after Mass?

After communion, any hosts that are left over are kept until the next Mass. Because these hosts have been consecrated (blessed), we believe they are the Body of Jesus.

They are kept in a ciborium in the *tabernacle*, near the altar. The tabernacle should be beautiful in honour of Jesus, our Saviour.

Using a tabernacle goes back to the time of Moses. The word "tabernacle" means "tent" or "dwelling place." In Jewish history, the tent housed the Ark of the Covenant, which held the Ten Commandments. The tabernacle was the symbol of God's presence with the people of Israel. When Solomon built the first Temple in Jerusalem, it included a tabernacle (no longer a tent) that was divided into two rooms: the Holy and the Holy of Holies, where the Ark was placed. The people saw the tabernacle as the most important symbol of their relationship with God: the covenant. Christians see Jesus Christ as the new covenant. Today, we consider this small cabinet, where we keep the Body of Christ, a holy place.

- Many people pray at the tabernacle in a church before or after Mass because the Body of Christ is stored here. If someone can't come to church for Mass because they are sick, the priest or a minister of communion will take a host from the tabernacle and bring it to the person along with prayers from the community.

- Another sign that the tabernacle is a holy place is that a *vigil candle* is always lit near it when the Body of Christ is present.

- The word "tabernacle" comes from the Latin word meaning small tent.

Why do churches have different names?

We can tell one church from another by their names. Having a name gives a church an identity, the same way your name gives you an identity. Just as you are more than "boy" or "girl," your parish church is more than "Roman Catholic church." This identity connects us with the sacred.

A church is named after one of these individuals or groups:

- the Blessed Trinity (for example, Blessed Trinity Catholic Church);

- our Lord Jesus Christ – either an event of his life or one of his titles (for example, Transfiguration of Our Lord Catholic Church, Holy Redeemer Catholic Church);

- the Holy Spirit (for example, Holy Spirit Catholic Church);

- the Blessed Virgin Mary – either an event in her life or one of her titles (for example, Annunciation of the Blessed Virgin Mary Catholic Church, Our Lady of Sorrows Catholic Church);

- one or more of the angels (for example, St. Gabriel Catholic Church, Holy Angels Catholic Church) or
- a saint (for example, St. Peter Catholic Church, St. Marguerite Bourgeoys Catholic Church)
- with special permission, a person who is designated "Blessed" (for example, Blessed Kateri Tekakwitha Catholic Church).

Names of churches can tell you a lot about the cultural heritage of a community. In the Archdiocese of Toronto, nine churches are dedicated to St. Patrick, the patron saint of Ireland. Many of the first Catholic immigrants to the area around Toronto were from Ireland.

When religious orders such as the Franciscans build churches, those churches may be named after their founders or saints (for example, St. Francis of Assisi, St. Clare).

Why *do churches have spires?*

Above the roofs of many of our churches are tall spires that point to the skies. At the top of the spire we usually find a cross.

Spires have been used for many centuries for different reasons. People used to think that God's home was in the skies. In pointing upwards, spires seem to show us that our lives should be directed towards heaven.

A spire is also a sign of a church's importance in a community. At one time, most people lived in villages and the nearby countryside. The church spire was usually the tallest thing in the village. People took pride in having a beautiful church with a tall spire. It also helped people who lived outside the village to feel connected with the church.

In earlier days of the Church in Europe, the countryside was not always a safe place. Raiders sometimes attacked the villages. Stone towers were built to protect the people. These towers became known as steeples. They also served as bell towers. Large bells would be rung to let people know it was time for Mass or other prayers. This was long before people had watches and clocks. The people depended on the bells to let them know when to gather.

Instead of towers, some churches have domes on their roofs. These had the same function as towers, but were more resistant to earthquakes and could cover a larger area. St. Peter's Basilica in Rome is an outstanding example of a domed church.

ST. PETER'S BASILICA IN ROME

25 Questions... About What We See in a Catholic Church

When it is completed, the spire of Barcelona's Sacrada Familia (Holy Family) Basilica will be 170 metres tall, making it the tallest church in the world. Cologne Cathedral in Germany is currently the world's tallest Catholic cathedral.

The tallest Catholic church in the Americas is St. Joseph's Oratory in Montreal (129 metres). It is topped with a dome and a cross.

Why are some churches built in the shape of a cross?

Viewed from the skies or from surrounding hills, the cross shape of many traditional churches is easy to see. The cross is the most recognizable symbol of Christianity because Jesus Christ suffered and died on a cross. But the cross is also the symbol of Christ's victory over death. It is not surprising, then, that our churches often use the shape of the cross in their design. The cross has a vertical line that reaches up into the heavens and connects people to God. It also has a horizontal line that connects us to each other. The Gospels tell us to love God and love our neighbours as ourselves. The cross is a symbol of this love.

Most traditional churches have a long central hall – the vertical part of the cross when seen from above. This part is the *nave* (see Question 6 for more about the nave). As we walk down the nave and approach the altar, the area widens. We have reached the part where the vertical part meets the horizontal part of the cross. This is called the *transept*.

At one time, churches were built so the people faced Jerusalem. Jerusalem was where Jesus died and then rose again. The priest spent most of the Mass with his back to the people so he could face Jerusalem, too.

Some modern churches emphasize that the Church is a community. They are built in a semi-circular or circular pattern that is focused on the altar.

After the Second Vatican Council (1962–1965), the Mass was revised. After these changes, the priest faced the people during the Mass.

?????????? **25** ?????????????

What do we call the people who go to church?

People go to Mass to worship God, so we call them *worshippers* in this book. Together they are the *assembly* or the *congregation*. St. Paul called worshippers the *Body of Christ*. Others call them the *Church*. People who belong to the parish church are called *parishioners*.

Around the world, people of different cultures and languages all worship in the same way. Their churches may have unique designs and be different sizes, but they all have the same basic elements described in this book. No matter where you go to Mass, you will notice the features of a Catholic church.

The Mass will be celebrated using the same scripture readings and the same basic prayers, too. Think about it: the prayers and readings have been said for centuries and are being said around the world right now. This is a powerful way in which Catholics are united to each other spiritually.

Wherever they live, worshippers feel united when they pray together, sing together and say the responses together. Worshipping God as a community helps people strengthen their relationship with God and gives them a sense of belonging. People are meant to be together. What is more beautiful than people joining together to be with God?

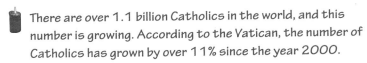 There are over 1.1 billion Catholics in the world, and this number is growing. According to the Vatican, the number of Catholics has grown by over 11% since the year 2000.

Some worshippers have special roles in the Church. If they are not priests or deacons, they are called lay ministers. Some of their work includes leading the singing, proclaiming the scriptures, bringing up the gifts, helping the priest give communion, teaching religious education, helping people to their pews, and visiting the sick.

WORDS TO KNOW

Advent: The beginning of the Church year, when we prepare for Christmas.

Aisle: A passageway between sections of pews.

Altar linen: Cloths used in worship made from a fabric called linen.

Ambo: The stand from where the scriptures are proclaimed.

Archbishop: The Bishop in a large area called an archdiocese.

Aspergillum: The object used to sprinkle water over the worshippers.

Assembly: Those who gather for Mass or other prayers.

Bishop: The priest who oversees an area called a diocese.

Body of Christ: One of the names for the community of Christian believers.

Calvary: The place in Jerusalem where Jesus was crucified.

Cathedra: The chair upon which the Bishop sits. It gives us the word "cathedral."

Censer: The object used to spread the smoke from burning incense.

Chalice: The cup used to hold the Blood of Christ at the Eucharist.

Ciborium: The bowl used to hold the Body of Christ (the hosts) during the Eucharist and in the tabernacle.

Congregation: Another word for the assembly.

Corporeal: The altar linen that is placed on the altar to catch fragments of the host.

Credence table: The small table where the vessels and gifts are placed until they are used during the Eucharist.

Cruets: Containers of wine and water that are brought to the altar before the Eucharistic Prayer.

Deacon: A man who may be married and who has been ordained to serve God's people.

Font: The basin or pool where baptisms take place. The water in it is blessed by the priest.

Genuflect: Going down on one knee as a form of prayer.

Lectern: A stand at the front of the church from which the Prayer of the Faithful is prayed and announcements are made.

Lectionary: The book of readings from the Bible that are used at Mass.

Lent: The 40 days of preparation before Easter.

Liturgy: Public acts of worship.

Martyr: A Christian who has died for his or her faith.

Nave: The central part of the church where most of the worshippers sit.

Ordinary Time: The times of the Church year between (1) the Baptism of the Lord and Lent and (2) the feast of the Body and Blood of Christ and Advent.

Parish: A church community within a diocese.

Paschal: Another word for Easter. "Paschal" comes from *pesach*, the Hebrew word for Passover.

Paten: A shallow, saucer-like object that is sometimes used to hold the Body of Christ in the Eucharist.

Pentecost: The feast that celebrates the coming of the Holy Spirit among the Apostles and Mary.

Pontius Pilate: The Roman prefect (leader) who oversaw Jesus' trial.

Purificator: The altar linen used to clean the chalice.

Rite of Christian Initiation of Adults (RCIA): A series of classes for people who want to become members of the Catholic Church.

Sacrament: An action that shows God's love in a very strong way. There are seven official sacraments of the Roman Catholic Church: Baptism, Eucharist, Reconciliation, Confirmation, Marriage, Holy Orders (priesthood), and Anointing of the Sick.

Sacramentary: The book that contains the prayers of the Mass.

Sanctuary: The part of the church around the altar.

Second Vatican Council: The gathering of the world's Bishops from 1962 to 1965, where a number of changes were made in the Church, including how we celebrate Mass.

Stoup: A small bowl of holy water found just inside the church.

Tabernacle: The place where the Body of Christ is kept after Mass.

Trinity: One God in three persons: Father, Son and Holy Spirit.

Vestments: The special clothing worn by the priest and the deacon.

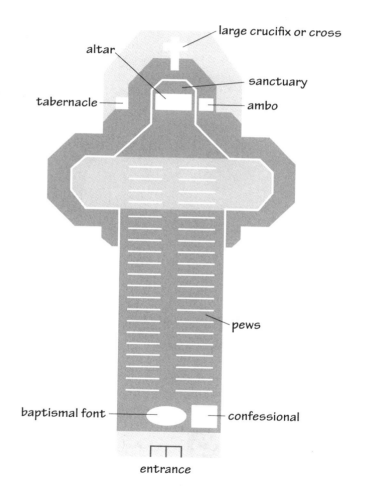

large crucifix or cross

altar

sanctuary

tabernacle

ambo

pews

baptismal font

confessional

entrance

Printed on Silva Enviro 100% post-consumer EcoLogo certified paper, processed chlorine free and manufactured using biogas energy.

    BIO GAS ENERGY